I0816554
LIFE BEGINS AT THE
End
OF YOUR COMFORT
ZONE
1978
ADVENTURE
TIME
ALL GOOD THINGS
ARE WILD AND FREE
OUTDOOR ADVENTURE
ADVENTURE AWAITS
AND I MUST GO

THIS JOURNAL BELONGS TO

____

HOW TO USE THIS BOOK

WELCOME TO YOUR JOURNAL, a place to prepare for upcoming camping trips, reflect on your best (and not-so-great) camping experiences, and keep notes for the future.

This journal is divided into three parts. The first part, Camping Logs, is the heart of the journal and your place to record details about every camping trip. Keep track of your favorite campsites (or coordinates when you venture off grid) and record the weather conditions of your trip, who you were with, and the sights you saw. Each log has guided prompts for key information, plus a section you can use to record highlights and observations. Designate a Log # for each trip to correlate with your entries in the Camping Log Index found on pages 6–9. This way, every trip will be easy to find and reference.

Following the logs, there are blank pages where you can include more notes, sketches, or etchings. Map your favorite trail, keep a running camp-supply list, or just reminisce about a particularly memorable camping adventure.

The final section, Camping Checklists, gives you a place to track your favorite camping trips, your camping bucket list, essential camping gear, meals, and notable flora and fauna. Now all you need is an open stretch of trail and a patch of earth to call yours for the night.

HAPPY CAMPING!

CAMPING LOGS

CAMPING LOG INDEX

LOG #	LOCATION	DATE

LOG#	LOCATION	DATE

CAMPING LOG INDEX

LOG #	LOCATION	DATE

LOG #	LOCATION	DATE

CAMPING LOG

LOG #

DATES

LOCATION

GPS COORDINATES/CAMPSITE # ______

ELEVATION/TERRAIN ______

WEATHER ______

______

ROUTE TAKEN TO CAMPSITE ______

______

FEES/PERMITS REQUIRED ______

PREFERRED SITE NUMBER(S) for next time ______

AMENITIES

- [ ] Parking | Number of vehicles ___
- [ ] Wheelchair accessibility
- [ ] Raised platform for tents
- [ ] Cell phone reception
- [ ] Campfire ring
- [ ] Grill
- [ ] Picnic table
- [ ] Firewood for sale

On-site trails: [ ] Biking [ ] Hiking [ ] ATV

Utility hook ups: [ ] Electric [ ] Water [ ] Sewer

Toilets: [ ] Pits [ ] Flush [ ] None

NOTES

______

______

______

______

MEALS

FLORA

FAUNA

HIGHLIGHTS/OBSERVATIONS

OVERALL RATING 

CAMPING LOG

LOG #

DATES

LOCATION

GPS COORDINATES/CAMPSITE # ______

ELEVATION/TERRAIN ______

WEATHER ______

______

ROUTE TAKEN TO CAMPSITE ______

______

FEES/PERMITS REQUIRED ______

PREFERRED SITE NUMBER(S) for next time ______

AMENITIES

- [ ] Parking | Number of vehicles ___
- [ ] Wheelchair accessibility
- [ ] Raised platform for tents
- [ ] Cell phone reception
- [ ] Campfire ring
- [ ] Grill
- [ ] Picnic table
- [ ] Firewood for sale

On-site trails: [ ] Biking [ ] Hiking [ ] ATV

Utility hook ups: [ ] Electric [ ] Water [ ] Sewer

Toilets: [ ] Pits [ ] Flush [ ] None

NOTES

MEALS

FLORA

FAUNA

HIGHLIGHTS/OBSERVATIONS

OVERALL RATING     

CAMPING LOG

LOG #

DATES **LOCATION**

GPS COORDINATES/CAMPSITE # ______

ELEVATION/TERRAIN ______

WEATHER ______

______

ROUTE TAKEN TO CAMPSITE ______

______

FEES/PERMITS REQUIRED ______

PREFERRED SITE NUMBER(S) for next time ______

AMENITIES

- [ ] Parking | Number of vehicles ___
- [ ] Wheelchair accessibility
- [ ] Raised platform for tents
- [ ] Cell phone reception
- [ ] Campfire ring
- [ ] Grill
- [ ] Picnic table
- [ ] Firewood for sale

On-site trails: [ ] Biking [ ] Hiking [ ] ATV

Utility hook ups: [ ] Electric [ ] Water [ ] Sewer

Toilets: [ ] Pits [ ] Flush [ ] None

NOTES

MEALS

FLORA

FAUNA

HIGHLIGHTS/OBSERVATIONS

CAMPING LOG

LOG #

DATES

LOCATION

GPS COORDINATES/CAMPSITE # ____________________

ELEVATION/TERRAIN ____________________

WEATHER ____________________

____

ROUTE TAKEN TO CAMPSITE ____________________

____

FEES/PERMITS REQUIRED ____________________

PREFERRED SITE NUMBER(S) for next time ____________________

AMENITIES

☐ Parking | Number of vehicles ___		☐ Wheelchair accessibility	
☐ Raised platform for tents		☐ Cell phone reception	
☐ Campfire ring	☐ Grill	☐ Picnic table	☐ Firewood for sale
On-site trails:	☐ Biking	☐ Hiking	☐ ATV
Utility hook ups:	☐ Electric	☐ Water	☐ Sewer
Toilets:	☐ Pits	☐ Flush	☐ None

NOTES

MEALS

FLORA

FAUNA

HIGHLIGHTS/OBSERVATIONS

OVERALL RATING     

CAMPING LOG

LOG #

DATES

LOCATION

GPS COORDINATES/CAMPSITE # ______

ELEVATION/TERRAIN ______

WEATHER ______

______

ROUTE TAKEN TO CAMPSITE ______

______

FEES/PERMITS REQUIRED ______

PREFERRED SITE NUMBER(S) for next time ______

AMENTIES

- [ ] Parking | Number of vehicles ___
- [ ] Wheelchair accessibility
- [ ] Raised platform for tents
- [ ] Cell phone reception
- [ ] Campfire ring
- [ ] Grill
- [ ] Picnic table
- [ ] Firewood for sale

On-site trails: [ ] Biking [ ] Hiking [ ] ATV

Utility hook ups: [ ] Electric [ ] Water [ ] Sewer

Toilets: [ ] Pits [ ] Flush [ ] None

NOTES

______

______

______

______

______

MEALS

FLORA

FAUNA

HIGHLIGHTS/OBSERVATIONS

OVERALL RATING     

CAMPING LOG

LOG #

DATES

LOCATION

GPS COORDINATES/CAMPSITE # ________

ELEVATION/TERRAIN ________

WEATHER ________

ROUTE TAKEN TO CAMPSITE ________

FEES/PERMITS REQUIRED ________

PREFERRED SITE NUMBER(S) for next time ________

AMENITIES

- [ ] Parking | Number of vehicles ___
- [ ] Wheelchair accessibility
- [ ] Raised platform for tents
- [ ] Cell phone reception
- [ ] Campfire ring
- [ ] Grill
- [ ] Picnic table
- [ ] Firewood for sale

On-site trails: [ ] Biking [ ] Hiking [ ] ATV

Utility hook ups: [ ] Electric [ ] Water [ ] Sewer

Toilets: [ ] Pits [ ] Flush [ ] None

NOTES

MEALS

FLORA

FAUNA

HIGHLIGHTS/OBSERVATIONS

OVERALL RATING

CAMPING LOG

LOG #

DATES **LOCATION**

GPS COORDINATES/CAMPSITE # ______

ELEVATION/TERRAIN ______

WEATHER ______

______

ROUTE TAKEN TO CAMPSITE ______

______

FEES/PERMITS REQUIRED ______

PREFERRED SITE NUMBER(S) for next time ______

AMENITIES

- [ ] Parking | Number of vehicles ___
- [ ] Wheelchair accessibility
- [ ] Raised platform for tents
- [ ] Cell phone reception
- [ ] Campfire ring
- [ ] Grill
- [ ] Picnic table
- [ ] Firewood for sale

On-site trails: [ ] Biking [ ] Hiking [ ] ATV

Utility hook ups: [ ] Electric [ ] Water [ ] Sewer

Toilets: [ ] Pits [ ] Flush [ ] None

NOTES

MEALS

FLORA

FAUNA

HIGHLIGHTS/OBSERVATIONS

CAMPING LOG

LOG #

DATES LOCATION

GPS COORDINATES/CAMPSITE # ______

ELEVATION/TERRAIN ______

WEATHER ______

______

ROUTE TAKEN TO CAMPSITE ______

______

FEES/PERMITS REQUIRED ______

PREFERRED SITE NUMBER(S) for next time ______

AMENITIES

- ☐ Parking | Number of vehicles ___
- ☐ Wheelchair accessibility
- ☐ Raised platform for tents
- ☐ Cell phone reception
- ☐ Campfire ring ☐ Grill ☐ Picnic table ☐ Firewood for sale

On-site trails: ☐ Biking ☐ Hiking ☐ ATV

Utility hook ups: ☐ Electric ☐ Water ☐ Sewer

Toilets: ☐ Pits ☐ Flush ☐ None

NOTES

______

MEALS

FLORA

FAUNA

HIGHLIGHTS/OBSERVATIONS

CAMPING LOG

LOG #

DATES

LOCATION

GPS COORDINATES/CAMPSITE # ______

ELEVATION/TERRAIN ______

WEATHER ______

______

ROUTE TAKEN TO CAMPSITE ______

______

FEES/PERMITS REQUIRED ______

PREFERRED SITE NUMBER(S) for next time ______

AMENITIES

- ☐ Parking | Number of vehicles ___
- ☐ Wheelchair accessibility
- ☐ Raised platform for tents
- ☐ Cell phone reception
- ☐ Campfire ring
- ☐ Grill
- ☐ Picnic table
- ☐ Firewood for sale

On-site trails: ☐ Biking ☐ Hiking ☐ ATV

Utility hook ups: ☐ Electric ☐ Water ☐ Sewer

Toilets: ☐ Pits ☐ Flush ☐ None

NOTES

MEALS

FLORA

FAUNA

HIGHLIGHTS/OBSERVATIONS

CAMPING LOG

LOG #

DATES

LOCATION

GPS COORDINATES/CAMPSITE # ______

ELEVATION/TERRAIN ______

WEATHER ______

______

ROUTE TAKEN TO CAMPSITE ______

______

FEES/PERMITS REQUIRED ______

PREFERRED SITE NUMBER(S) for next time ______

AMENITIES

- [ ] Parking | Number of vehicles ___
- [ ] Wheelchair accessibility
- [ ] Raised platform for tents
- [ ] Cell phone reception
- [ ] Campfire ring
- [ ] Grill
- [ ] Picnic table
- [ ] Firewood for sale

On-site trails: [ ] Biking [ ] Hiking [ ] ATV

Utility hook ups: [ ] Electric [ ] Water [ ] Sewer

Toilets: [ ] Pits [ ] Flush [ ] None

NOTES

______

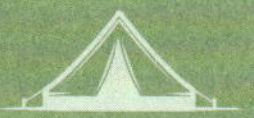

MEALS

FLORA

FAUNA

HIGHLIGHTS/OBSERVATIONS

CAMPING LOG

LOG #

DATES

LOCATION

GPS COORDINATES/CAMPSITE # ______

ELEVATION/TERRAIN ______

WEATHER ______

______

ROUTE TAKEN TO CAMPSITE ______

______

FEES/PERMITS REQUIRED ______

PREFERRED SITE NUMBER(S) for next time ______

AMENITIES

- [ ] Parking | Number of vehicles ___
- [ ] Wheelchair accessibility
- [ ] Raised platform for tents
- [ ] Cell phone reception
- [ ] Campfire ring
- [ ] Grill
- [ ] Picnic table
- [ ] Firewood for sale

On-site trails: [ ] Biking [ ] Hiking [ ] ATV

Utility hook ups: [ ] Electric [ ] Water [ ] Sewer

Toilets: [ ] Pits [ ] Flush [ ] None

NOTES

MEALS

FLORA

FAUNA

HIGHLIGHTS/OBSERVATIONS

CAMPING LOG

LOG #

DATES

LOCATION

GPS COORDINATES/CAMPSITE # ______

ELEVATION/TERRAIN ______

WEATHER ______

ROUTE TAKEN TO CAMPSITE ______

FEES/PERMITS REQUIRED ______

PREFERRED SITE NUMBER(S) for next time ______

AMENITIES

- [ ] Parking | Number of vehicles ___
- [ ] Wheelchair accessibility
- [ ] Raised platform for tents
- [ ] Cell phone reception
- [ ] Campfire ring
- [ ] Grill
- [ ] Picnic table
- [ ] Firewood for sale

On-site trails: [ ] Biking [ ] Hiking [ ] ATV

Utility hook ups: [ ] Electric [ ] Water [ ] Sewer

Toilets: [ ] Pits [ ] Flush [ ] None

NOTES

MEALS

FLORA

FAUNA

HIGHLIGHTS/OBSERVATIONS

OVERALL RATING     

CAMPING LOG

LOG #

DATES

LOCATION

GPS COORDINATES/CAMPSITE # ______

ELEVATION/TERRAIN ______

WEATHER ______

______

ROUTE TAKEN TO CAMPSITE ______

______

FEES/PERMITS REQUIRED ______

PREFERRED SITE NUMBER(S) for next time ______

AMENITIES

- [ ] Parking | Number of vehicles ___
- [ ] Wheelchair accessibility
- [ ] Raised platform for tents
- [ ] Cell phone reception
- [ ] Campfire ring
- [ ] Grill
- [ ] Picnic table
- [ ] Firewood for sale

On-site trails: [ ] Biking [ ] Hiking [ ] ATV

Utility hook ups: [ ] Electric [ ] Water [ ] Sewer

Toilets: [ ] Pits [ ] Flush [ ] None

NOTES

______

MEALS

FLORA

FAUNA

HIGHLIGHTS/OBSERVATIONS

CAMPING LOG

LOG #

DATES

LOCATION

GPS COORDINATES/CAMPSITE # ______

ELEVATION/TERRAIN ______

WEATHER ______

______

ROUTE TAKEN TO CAMPSITE ______

______

FEES/PERMITS REQUIRED ______

PREFERRED SITE NUMBER(S) for next time ______

AMENITIES

- [ ] Parking | Number of vehicles ___
- [ ] Wheelchair accessibility
- [ ] Raised platform for tents
- [ ] Cell phone reception
- [ ] Campfire ring
- [ ] Grill
- [ ] Picnic table
- [ ] Firewood for sale

On-site trails: [ ] Biking [ ] Hiking [ ] ATV

Utility hook ups: [ ] Electric [ ] Water [ ] Sewer

Toilets: [ ] Pits [ ] Flush [ ] None

NOTES

______

______

______

______

MEALS

FLORA

FAUNA

HIGHLIGHTS/OBSERVATIONS

CAMPING LOG

LOG #

DATES

LOCATION

GPS COORDINATES/CAMPSITE #

ELEVATION/TERRAIN

WEATHER

ROUTE TAKEN TO CAMPSITE

FEES/PERMITS REQUIRED

PREFERRED SITE NUMBER(S) for next time

AMENITIES

- ☐ Parking | Number of vehicles ___
- ☐ Wheelchair accessibility
- ☐ Raised platform for tents
- ☐ Cell phone reception
- ☐ Campfire ring
- ☐ Grill
- ☐ Picnic table
- ☐ Firewood for sale

On-site trails: ☐ Biking ☐ Hiking ☐ ATV

Utility hook ups: ☐ Electric ☐ Water ☐ Sewer

Toilets: ☐ Pits ☐ Flush ☐ None

NOTES

MEALS

FLORA

FAUNA

HIGHLIGHTS/OBSERVATIONS

CAMPING LOG

LOG #

DATES

LOCATION

GPS COORDINATES/CAMPSITE # ______

ELEVATION/TERRAIN ______

WEATHER ______

______

ROUTE TAKEN TO CAMPSITE ______

______

FEES/PERMITS REQUIRED ______

PREFERRED SITE NUMBER(S) for next time ______

AMENITIES

- [ ] Parking | Number of vehicles ___
- [ ] Wheelchair accessibility
- [ ] Raised platform for tents
- [ ] Cell phone reception
- [ ] Campfire ring
- [ ] Grill
- [ ] Picnic table
- [ ] Firewood for sale

On-site trails: [ ] Biking [ ] Hiking [ ] ATV

Utility hook ups: [ ] Electric [ ] Water [ ] Sewer

Toilets: [ ] Pits [ ] Flush [ ] None

NOTES

______

MEALS

FLORA

FAUNA

HIGHLIGHTS/OBSERVATIONS

CAMPING LOG

LOG #

DATES

LOCATION

GPS COORDINATES/CAMPSITE # ______

ELEVATION/TERRAIN ______

WEATHER ______

ROUTE TAKEN TO CAMPSITE ______

FEES/PERMITS REQUIRED ______

PREFERRED SITE NUMBER(S) for next time ______

AMENITIES

- [ ] Parking | Number of vehicles ___
- [ ] Wheelchair accessibility
- [ ] Raised platform for tents
- [ ] Cell phone reception
- [ ] Campfire ring
- [ ] Grill
- [ ] Picnic table
- [ ] Firewood for sale

On-site trails: [ ] Biking [ ] Hiking [ ] ATV

Utility hook ups: [ ] Electric [ ] Water [ ] Sewer

Toilets: [ ] Pits [ ] Flush [ ] None

NOTES

MEALS

FLORA

FAUNA

HIGHLIGHTS/OBSERVATIONS

CAMPING LOG

LOG #

DATES

LOCATION

GPS COORDINATES/CAMPSITE # ______

ELEVATION/TERRAIN ______

WEATHER ______

______

ROUTE TAKEN TO CAMPSITE ______

______

FEES/PERMITS REQUIRED ______

PREFERRED SITE NUMBER(S) for next time ______

AMENITIES

☐ Parking | Number of vehicles ___		☐ Wheelchair accessibility	
☐ Raised platform for tents		☐ Cell phone reception	
☐ Campfire ring	☐ Grill	☐ Picnic table	☐ Firewood for sale
On-site trails:	☐ Biking	☐ Hiking	☐ ATV
Utility hook ups:	☐ Electric	☐ Water	☐ Sewer
Toilets:	☐ Pits	☐ Flush	☐ None

NOTES

______

______

______

______

MEALS

FLORA

FAUNA

HIGHLIGHTS/OBSERVATIONS

CAMPING LOG

LOG #

DATES

LOCATION

GPS COORDINATES/CAMPSITE # ______

ELEVATION/TERRAIN ______

WEATHER ______

______

ROUTE TAKEN TO CAMPSITE ______

______

FEES/PERMITS REQUIRED ______

PREFERRED SITE NUMBER(S) for next time ______

AMENITIES

☐ Parking | Number of vehicles ___		☐ Wheelchair accessibility	
☐ Raised platform for tents		☐ Cell phone reception	
☐ Campfire ring	☐ Grill	☐ Picnic table	☐ Firewood for sale
On-site trails:	☐ Biking	☐ Hiking	☐ ATV
Utility hook ups:	☐ Electric	☐ Water	☐ Sewer
Toilets:	☐ Pits	☐ Flush	☐ None

NOTES

______

______

______

______

MEALS

FLORA

FAUNA

HIGHLIGHTS/OBSERVATIONS

OVERALL RATING     

CAMPING LOG

LOG #

DATES

LOCATION

GPS COORDINATES/CAMPSITE # ______

ELEVATION/TERRAIN ______

WEATHER ______

ROUTE TAKEN TO CAMPSITE ______

FEES/PERMITS REQUIRED ______

PREFERRED SITE NUMBER(S) for next time ______

AMENITIES

- [ ] Parking | Number of vehicles ___
- [ ] Wheelchair accessibility
- [ ] Raised platform for tents
- [ ] Cell phone reception
- [ ] Campfire ring
- [ ] Grill
- [ ] Picnic table
- [ ] Firewood for sale

On-site trails: [ ] Biking [ ] Hiking [ ] ATV

Utility hook ups: [ ] Electric [ ] Water [ ] Sewer

Toilets: [ ] Pits [ ] Flush [ ] None

NOTES

MEALS

FLORA

FAUNA

HIGHLIGHTS/OBSERVATIONS

CAMPING LOG

LOG #

DATES

LOCATION

GPS COORDINATES/CAMPSITE # ____________________

ELEVATION/TERRAIN ____________________

WEATHER ____________________

____

ROUTE TAKEN TO CAMPSITE ____________________

____

FEES/PERMITS REQUIRED ____________________

PREFERRED SITE NUMBER(S) for next time ____________________

AMENITIES

☐ Parking | Number of vehicles ___		☐ Wheelchair accessibility	
☐ Raised platform for tents		☐ Cell phone reception	
☐ Campfire ring	☐ Grill	☐ Picnic table	☐ Firewood for sale
On-site trails:	☐ Biking	☐ Hiking	☐ ATV
Utility hook ups:	☐ Electric	☐ Water	☐ Sewer
Toilets:	☐ Pits	☐ Flush	☐ None

NOTES

____

MEALS

FLORA

FAUNA

HIGHLIGHTS/OBSERVATIONS

OVERALL RATING     

CAMPING LOG

LOG #

DATES

LOCATION

GPS COORDINATES/CAMPSITE # ______

ELEVATION/TERRAIN ______

WEATHER ______

______

ROUTE TAKEN TO CAMPSITE ______

______

FEES/PERMITS REQUIRED ______

PREFERRED SITE NUMBER(S) for next time ______

AMENITIES

- [ ] Parking | Number of vehicles ___
- [ ] Wheelchair accessibility
- [ ] Raised platform for tents
- [ ] Cell phone reception
- [ ] Campfire ring
- [ ] Grill
- [ ] Picnic table
- [ ] Firewood for sale

On-site trails: [ ] Biking [ ] Hiking [ ] ATV

Utility hook ups: [ ] Electric [ ] Water [ ] Sewer

Toilets: [ ] Pits [ ] Flush [ ] None

NOTES

______

MEALS

FLORA

FAUNA

HIGHLIGHTS/OBSERVATIONS

CAMPING LOG

LOG #

DATES

LOCATION

GPS COORDINATES/CAMPSITE # ____

ELEVATION/TERRAIN ____

WEATHER ____

____

ROUTE TAKEN TO CAMPSITE ____

____

FEES/PERMITS REQUIRED ____

PREFERRED SITE NUMBER(S) for next time ____

AMENITIES

- [ ] Parking | Number of vehicles ___
- [ ] Wheelchair accessibility
- [ ] Raised platform for tents
- [ ] Cell phone reception
- [ ] Campfire ring
- [ ] Grill
- [ ] Picnic table
- [ ] Firewood for sale

On-site trails: [ ] Biking [ ] Hiking [ ] ATV

Utility hook ups: [ ] Electric [ ] Water [ ] Sewer

Toilets: [ ] Pits [ ] Flush [ ] None

NOTES

____

MEALS

FLORA

FAUNA

HIGHLIGHTS/OBSERVATIONS

CAMPING LOG

LOG #

DATES

LOCATION

GPS COORDINATES/CAMPSITE # ______

ELEVATION/TERRAIN ______

WEATHER ______

______

ROUTE TAKEN TO CAMPSITE ______

______

FEES/PERMITS REQUIRED ______

PREFERRED SITE NUMBER(S) for next time ______

AMENITIES

☐ Parking | Number of vehicles ___		☐ Wheelchair accessibility	
☐ Raised platform for tents		☐ Cell phone reception	
☐ Campfire ring	☐ Grill	☐ Picnic table	☐ Firewood for sale
On-site trails:	☐ Biking	☐ Hiking	☐ ATV
Utility hook ups:	☐ Electric	☐ Water	☐ Sewer
Toilets:	☐ Pits	☐ Flush	☐ None

NOTES

______

______

______

______

MEALS

FLORA

FAUNA

HIGHLIGHTS/OBSERVATIONS

CAMPING LOG

LOG #

DATES

LOCATION

GPS COORDINATES/CAMPSITE # ______

ELEVATION/TERRAIN ______

WEATHER ______

ROUTE TAKEN TO CAMPSITE ______

FEES/PERMITS REQUIRED ______

PREFERRED SITE NUMBER(S) for next time ______

AMENITIES

- [ ] Parking | Number of vehicles ___
- [ ] Wheelchair accessibility
- [ ] Raised platform for tents
- [ ] Cell phone reception
- [ ] Campfire ring
- [ ] Grill
- [ ] Picnic table
- [ ] Firewood for sale

On-site trails: [ ] Biking [ ] Hiking [ ] ATV

Utility hook ups: [ ] Electric [ ] Water [ ] Sewer

Toilets: [ ] Pits [ ] Flush [ ] None

NOTES

MEALS

FLORA

FAUNA

HIGHLIGHTS/OBSERVATIONS

CAMPING LOG

LOG #

DATES

LOCATION

GPS COORDINATES/CAMPSITE # ______

ELEVATION/TERRAIN ______

WEATHER ______

______

ROUTE TAKEN TO CAMPSITE ______

______

FEES/PERMITS REQUIRED ______

PREFERRED SITE NUMBER(S) for next time ______

AMENITIES

- [ ] Parking | Number of vehicles ___
- [ ] Wheelchair accessibility
- [ ] Raised platform for tents
- [ ] Cell phone reception
- [ ] Campfire ring
- [ ] Grill
- [ ] Picnic table
- [ ] Firewood for sale

On-site trails: [ ] Biking [ ] Hiking [ ] ATV

Utility hook ups: [ ] Electric [ ] Water [ ] Sewer

Toilets: [ ] Pits [ ] Flush [ ] None

NOTES

MEALS

FLORA

FAUNA

HIGHLIGHTS/OBSERVATIONS

OVERALL RATING

CAMPING LOG

LOG #

DATES

LOCATION

GPS COORDINATES/CAMPSITE # __________

ELEVATION/TERRAIN __________

WEATHER __________

ROUTE TAKEN TO CAMPSITE __________

FEES/PERMITS REQUIRED __________

PREFERRED SITE NUMBER(S) for next time __________

AMENITIES

- ☐ Parking | Number of vehicles ___
- ☐ Wheelchair accessibility
- ☐ Raised platform for tents
- ☐ Cell phone reception
- ☐ Campfire ring
- ☐ Grill
- ☐ Picnic table
- ☐ Firewood for sale

On-site trails: ☐ Biking ☐ Hiking ☐ ATV

Utility hook ups: ☐ Electric ☐ Water ☐ Sewer

Toilets: ☐ Pits ☐ Flush ☐ None

NOTES

MEALS

FLORA

FAUNA

HIGHLIGHTS/OBSERVATIONS

OVERALL RATING     

CAMPING LOG

LOG #

DATES

LOCATION

GPS COORDINATES/CAMPSITE # ______

ELEVATION/TERRAIN ______

WEATHER ______

______

ROUTE TAKEN TO CAMPSITE ______

______

FEES/PERMITS REQUIRED ______

PREFERRED SITE NUMBER(S) for next time ______

AMENITIES

- [ ] Parking | Number of vehicles ___
- [ ] Wheelchair accessibility
- [ ] Raised platform for tents
- [ ] Cell phone reception
- [ ] Campfire ring
- [ ] Grill
- [ ] Picnic table
- [ ] Firewood for sale

On-site trails: [ ] Biking [ ] Hiking [ ] ATV

Utility hook ups: [ ] Electric [ ] Water [ ] Sewer

Toilets: [ ] Pits [ ] Flush [ ] None

NOTES

______

MEALS

FLORA

FAUNA

HIGHLIGHTS/OBSERVATIONS

OVERALL RATING     

CAMPING LOG

LOG #

DATES

LOCATION

GPS COORDINATES/CAMPSITE #

ELEVATION/TERRAIN

WEATHER

ROUTE TAKEN TO CAMPSITE

FEES/PERMITS REQUIRED

PREFERRED SITE NUMBER(S) for next time

AMENITIES

- [ ] Parking | Number of vehicles ___
- [ ] Wheelchair accessibility
- [ ] Raised platform for tents
- [ ] Cell phone reception
- [ ] Campfire ring
- [ ] Grill
- [ ] Picnic table
- [ ] Firewood for sale

On-site trails: [ ] Biking [ ] Hiking [ ] ATV

Utility hook ups: [ ] Electric [ ] Water [ ] Sewer

Toilets: [ ] Pits [ ] Flush [ ] None

NOTES

MEALS

FLORA

FAUNA

HIGHLIGHTS/OBSERVATIONS

OVERALL RATING     

CAMPING LOG

LOG #

DATES

LOCATION

GPS COORDINATES/CAMPSITE # ____

ELEVATION/TERRAIN ____

WEATHER ____

ROUTE TAKEN TO CAMPSITE ____

FEES/PERMITS REQUIRED ____

PREFERRED SITE NUMBER(S) for next time ____

AMENITIES

- [ ] Parking | Number of vehicles ___
- [ ] Wheelchair accessibility
- [ ] Raised platform for tents
- [ ] Cell phone reception
- [ ] Campfire ring
- [ ] Grill
- [ ] Picnic table
- [ ] Firewood for sale

On-site trails: [ ] Biking [ ] Hiking [ ] ATV

Utility hook ups: [ ] Electric [ ] Water [ ] Sewer

Toilets: [ ] Pits [ ] Flush [ ] None

NOTES

MEALS

FLORA

FAUNA

HIGHLIGHTS/OBSERVATIONS

CAMPING LOG

LOG #

DATES

LOCATION

GPS COORDINATES/CAMPSITE # ______

ELEVATION/TERRAIN ______

WEATHER ______

ROUTE TAKEN TO CAMPSITE ______

FEES/PERMITS REQUIRED ______

PREFERRED SITE NUMBER(S) for next time ______

AMENITIES

- [ ] Parking | Number of vehicles ___
- [ ] Wheelchair accessibility
- [ ] Raised platform for tents
- [ ] Cell phone reception
- [ ] Campfire ring
- [ ] Grill
- [ ] Picnic table
- [ ] Firewood for sale

On-site trails: [ ] Biking [ ] Hiking [ ] ATV

Utility hook ups: [ ] Electric [ ] Water [ ] Sewer

Toilets: [ ] Pits [ ] Flush [ ] None

NOTES

MEALS

FLORA

FAUNA

HIGHLIGHTS/OBSERVATIONS

CAMPING LOG

LOG #

DATES

LOCATION

GPS COORDINATES/CAMPSITE # ____

ELEVATION/TERRAIN ____

WEATHER ____

____

ROUTE TAKEN TO CAMPSITE ____

____

FEES/PERMITS REQUIRED ____

PREFERRED SITE NUMBER(S) for next time ____

AMENTIES

- ☐ Parking | Number of vehicles ___
- ☐ Wheelchair accessibility
- ☐ Raised platform for tents
- ☐ Cell phone reception
- ☐ Campfire ring ☐ Grill ☐ Picnic table ☐ Firewood for sale

On-site trails: ☐ Biking ☐ Hiking ☐ ATV

Utility hook ups: ☐ Electric ☐ Water ☐ Sewer

Toilets: ☐ Pits ☐ Flush ☐ None

NOTES

____

MEALS

FLORA

FAUNA

HIGHLIGHTS/OBSERVATIONS

OVERALL RATING     

CAMPING LOG

LOG #

DATES LOCATION

GPS COORDINATES/CAMPSITE # ____

ELEVATION/TERRAIN ____

WEATHER ____

____

ROUTE TAKEN TO CAMPSITE ____

____

FEES/PERMITS REQUIRED ____

PREFERRED SITE NUMBER(S) for next time ____

AMENITIES

Parking | Number of vehicles ___		Wheelchair accessibility	
Raised platform for tents		Cell phone reception	
Campfire ring	Grill	Picnic table	Firewood for sale
On-site trails:	Biking	Hiking	ATV
Utility hook ups:	Electric	Water	Sewer
Toilets:	Pits	Flush	None

NOTES

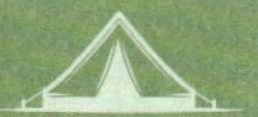

MEALS

FLORA

FAUNA

HIGHLIGHTS/OBSERVATIONS

CAMPING LOG

LOG #

DATES

LOCATION

GPS COORDINATES/CAMPSITE # ______

ELEVATION/TERRAIN ______

WEATHER ______

______

ROUTE TAKEN TO CAMPSITE ______

______

FEES/PERMITS REQUIRED ______

PREFERRED SITE NUMBER(S) for next time ______

AMENITIES

- [ ] Parking | Number of vehicles ___
- [ ] Wheelchair accessibility
- [ ] Raised platform for tents
- [ ] Cell phone reception
- [ ] Campfire ring
- [ ] Grill
- [ ] Picnic table
- [ ] Firewood for sale

On-site trails:

- [ ] Biking
- [ ] Hiking
- [ ] ATV

Utility hook ups:

- [ ] Electric
- [ ] Water
- [ ] Sewer

Toilets:

- [ ] Pits
- [ ] Flush
- [ ] None

NOTES ______

MEALS

FLORA

FAUNA

HIGHLIGHTS/OBSERVATIONS

CAMPING LOG

LOG #

DATES

LOCATION

GPS COORDINATES/CAMPSITE # ______

ELEVATION/TERRAIN ______

WEATHER ______

ROUTE TAKEN TO CAMPSITE ______

FEES/PERMITS REQUIRED ______

PREFERRED SITE NUMBER(S) for next time ______

AMENITIES

- ☐ Parking | Number of vehicles ___
- ☐ Wheelchair accessibility
- ☐ Raised platform for tents
- ☐ Cell phone reception
- ☐ Campfire ring ☐ Grill ☐ Picnic table ☐ Firewood for sale

On-site trails: ☐ Biking ☐ Hiking ☐ ATV

Utility hook ups: ☐ Electric ☐ Water ☐ Sewer

Toilets: ☐ Pits ☐ Flush ☐ None

NOTES

MEALS

FLORA

FAUNA

HIGHLIGHTS/OBSERVATIONS

CAMPING LOG

LOG #

DATES

LOCATION

GPS COORDINATES/CAMPSITE # ____________________

ELEVATION/TERRAIN ____________________

WEATHER ____________________

____

ROUTE TAKEN TO CAMPSITE ____________________

____

FEES/PERMITS REQUIRED ____________________

PREFERRED SITE NUMBER(S) for next time ____________________

AMENITIES

- [ ] Parking | Number of vehicles ___
- [ ] Wheelchair accessibility
- [ ] Raised platform for tents
- [ ] Cell phone reception
- [ ] Campfire ring
- [ ] Grill
- [ ] Picnic table
- [ ] Firewood for sale

On-site trails: [ ] Biking [ ] Hiking [ ] ATV

Utility hook ups: [ ] Electric [ ] Water [ ] Sewer

Toilets: [ ] Pits [ ] Flush [ ] None

NOTES

____

____

____

____

MEALS

FLORA

FAUNA

HIGHLIGHTS/OBSERVATIONS

CAMPING LOG

LOG #

DATES

LOCATION

GPS COORDINATES/CAMPSITE # ______

ELEVATION/TERRAIN ______

WEATHER ______

ROUTE TAKEN TO CAMPSITE ______

FEES/PERMITS REQUIRED ______

PREFERRED SITE NUMBER(S) for next time ______

AMENITIES

- ☐ Parking | Number of vehicles ___
- ☐ Wheelchair accessibility
- ☐ Raised platform for tents
- ☐ Cell phone reception
- ☐ Campfire ring
- ☐ Grill
- ☐ Picnic table
- ☐ Firewood for sale

On-site trails: ☐ Biking ☐ Hiking ☐ ATV

Utility hook ups: ☐ Electric ☐ Water ☐ Sewer

Toilets: ☐ Pits ☐ Flush ☐ None

NOTES

MEALS

FLORA

FAUNA

HIGHLIGHTS/OBSERVATIONS

OVERALL RATING      

CAMPING LOG

LOG #

DATES LOCATION

GPS COORDINATES/CAMPSITE # ____________________

ELEVATION/TERRAIN ____________________

WEATHER ____________________

____

ROUTE TAKEN TO CAMPSITE ____________________

____

FEES/PERMITS REQUIRED ____________________

PREFERRED SITE NUMBER(S) for next time ____________________

AMENITIES

- [ ] Parking | Number of vehicles ___
- [ ] Wheelchair accessibility
- [ ] Raised platform for tents
- [ ] Cell phone reception
- [ ] Campfire ring
- [ ] Grill
- [ ] Picnic table
- [ ] Firewood for sale

On-site trails: [ ] Biking [ ] Hiking [ ] ATV

Utility hook ups: [ ] Electric [ ] Water [ ] Sewer

Toilets: [ ] Pits [ ] Flush [ ] None

NOTES

MEALS

FLORA

FAUNA

HIGHLIGHTS/OBSERVATIONS

CAMPING LOG

LOG #

DATES LOCATION

GPS COORDINATES/CAMPSITE # ______

ELEVATION/TERRAIN ______

WEATHER ______

______

ROUTE TAKEN TO CAMPSITE ______

______

FEES/PERMITS REQUIRED ______

PREFERRED SITE NUMBER(S) for next time ______

AMENITIES

- ☐ Parking | Number of vehicles ___
- ☐ Wheelchair accessibility
- ☐ Raised platform for tents
- ☐ Cell phone reception
- ☐ Campfire ring ☐ Grill ☐ Picnic table ☐ Firewood for sale

On-site trails: ☐ Biking ☐ Hiking ☐ ATV

Utility hook ups: ☐ Electric ☐ Water ☐ Sewer

Toilets: ☐ Pits ☐ Flush ☐ None

NOTES

______

MEALS

FLORA

FAUNA

HIGHLIGHTS/OBSERVATIONS

CAMPING LOG

LOG #

DATES

LOCATION

GPS COORDINATES/CAMPSITE #

ELEVATION/TERRAIN

WEATHER

ROUTE TAKEN TO CAMPSITE

FEES/PERMITS REQUIRED

PREFERRED SITE NUMBER(S) for next time

AMENITIES

- Parking | Number of vehicles ___
- Wheelchair accessibility
- Raised platform for tents
- Cell phone reception
- Campfire ring
- Grill
- Picnic table
- Firewood for sale

On-site trails: Biking / Hiking / ATV

Utility hook ups: Electric / Water / Sewer

Toilets: Pits / Flush / None

NOTES

MEALS

FLORA

FAUNA

HIGHLIGHTS/OBSERVATIONS

CAMPING LOG

LOG #

DATES

LOCATION

GPS COORDINATES/CAMPSITE # ______

ELEVATION/TERRAIN ______

WEATHER ______

______

ROUTE TAKEN TO CAMPSITE ______

______

FEES/PERMITS REQUIRED ______

PREFERRED SITE NUMBER(S) for next time ______

AMENITIES

- [ ] Parking | Number of vehicles ___
- [ ] Wheelchair accessibility
- [ ] Raised platform for tents
- [ ] Cell phone reception
- [ ] Campfire ring
- [ ] Grill
- [ ] Picnic table
- [ ] Firewood for sale

On-site trails: [ ] Biking [ ] Hiking [ ] ATV

Utility hook ups: [ ] Electric [ ] Water [ ] Sewer

Toilets: [ ] Pits [ ] Flush [ ] None

NOTES

______

MEALS

FLORA

FAUNA

HIGHLIGHTS/OBSERVATIONS

CAMPING LOG

LOG #

DATES LOCATION

GPS COORDINATES/CAMPSITE # ____

ELEVATION/TERRAIN ____

WEATHER ____

ROUTE TAKEN TO CAMPSITE ____

FEES/PERMITS REQUIRED ____

PREFERRED SITE NUMBER(S) for next time ____

AMENITIES

- [ ] Parking | Number of vehicles ___
- [ ] Wheelchair accessibility
- [ ] Raised platform for tents
- [ ] Cell phone reception
- [ ] Campfire ring
- [ ] Grill
- [ ] Picnic table
- [ ] Firewood for sale

On-site trails: [ ] Biking [ ] Hiking [ ] ATV

Utility hook ups: [ ] Electric [ ] Water [ ] Sewer

Toilets: [ ] Pits [ ] Flush [ ] None

NOTES

MEALS

FLORA

FAUNA

HIGHLIGHTS/OBSERVATIONS

CAMPING LOG

LOG #

DATES

LOCATION

GPS COORDINATES/CAMPSITE # ______

ELEVATION/TERRAIN ______

WEATHER ______

______

ROUTE TAKEN TO CAMPSITE ______

______

FEES/PERMITS REQUIRED ______

PREFERRED SITE NUMBER(S) for next time ______

AMENITIES

- [ ] Parking | Number of vehicles ___
- [ ] Wheelchair accessibility
- [ ] Raised platform for tents
- [ ] Cell phone reception
- [ ] Campfire ring
- [ ] Grill
- [ ] Picnic table
- [ ] Firewood for sale

On-site trails: [ ] Biking [ ] Hiking [ ] ATV

Utility hook ups: [ ] Electric [ ] Water [ ] Sewer

Toilets: [ ] Pits [ ] Flush [ ] None

NOTES

MEALS

FLORA

FAUNA

HIGHLIGHTS/OBSERVATIONS

CAMPING LOG

LOG #

DATES

LOCATION

GPS COORDINATES/CAMPSITE # ______

ELEVATION/TERRAIN ______

WEATHER ______

______

ROUTE TAKEN TO CAMPSITE ______

______

FEES/PERMITS REQUIRED ______

PREFERRED SITE NUMBER(S) for next time ______

AMENITIES

- [ ] Parking | Number of vehicles ___
- [ ] Wheelchair accessibility
- [ ] Raised platform for tents
- [ ] Cell phone reception
- [ ] Campfire ring
- [ ] Grill
- [ ] Picnic table
- [ ] Firewood for sale

On-site trails: [ ] Biking [ ] Hiking [ ] ATV

Utility hook ups: [ ] Electric [ ] Water [ ] Sewer

Toilets: [ ] Pits [ ] Flush [ ] None

NOTES

MEALS

FLORA

FAUNA

HIGHLIGHTS/OBSERVATIONS

OVERALL RATING      

CAMPING LOG

LOG #

DATES

LOCATION

GPS COORDINATES/CAMPSITE # ______________________________

ELEVATION/TERRAIN ______________________________

WEATHER ______________________________

____

ROUTE TAKEN TO CAMPSITE ______________________________

____

FEES/PERMITS REQUIRED ______________________________

PREFERRED SITE NUMBER(S) for next time ______________________________

AMENITIES

- [ ] Parking | Number of vehicles ___
- [ ] Wheelchair accessibility
- [ ] Raised platform for tents
- [ ] Cell phone reception
- [ ] Campfire ring
- [ ] Grill
- [ ] Picnic table
- [ ] Firewood for sale

On-site trails: [ ] Biking [ ] Hiking [ ] ATV

Utility hook ups: [ ] Electric [ ] Water [ ] Sewer

Toilets: [ ] Pits [ ] Flush [ ] None

NOTES

____

____

____

____

MEALS

FLORA

FAUNA

HIGHLIGHTS/OBSERVATIONS

OVERALL RATING     

CAMPING LOG

LOG #

DATES

LOCATION

GPS COORDINATES/CAMPSITE # ____________________

ELEVATION/TERRAIN ____________________

WEATHER ____________________

____

ROUTE TAKEN TO CAMPSITE ____________________

____

FEES/PERMITS REQUIRED ____________________

PREFERRED SITE NUMBER(S) for next time ____________________

AMENITIES

- ☐ Parking | Number of vehicles ___
- ☐ Wheelchair accessibility
- ☐ Raised platform for tents
- ☐ Cell phone reception
- ☐ Campfire ring
- ☐ Grill
- ☐ Picnic table
- ☐ Firewood for sale

On-site trails: ☐ Biking ☐ Hiking ☐ ATV

Utility hook ups: ☐ Electric ☐ Water ☐ Sewer

Toilets: ☐ Pits ☐ Flush ☐ None

NOTES

____

MEALS

FLORA

FAUNA

HIGHLIGHTS/OBSERVATIONS

OVERALL RATING     

CAMPING LOG

LOG #

DATES

LOCATION

GPS COORDINATES/CAMPSITE # ______

ELEVATION/TERRAIN ______

WEATHER ______

______

ROUTE TAKEN TO CAMPSITE ______

______

FEES/PERMITS REQUIRED ______

PREFERRED SITE NUMBER(S) for next time ______

AMENITIES

- [ ] Parking | Number of vehicles ___
- [ ] Wheelchair accessibility
- [ ] Raised platform for tents
- [ ] Cell phone reception
- [ ] Campfire ring
- [ ] Grill
- [ ] Picnic table
- [ ] Firewood for sale

On-site trails: [ ] Biking [ ] Hiking [ ] ATV

Utility hook ups: [ ] Electric [ ] Water [ ] Sewer

Toilets: [ ] Pits [ ] Flush [ ] None

NOTES

______

______

______

______

MEALS

FLORA

FAUNA

HIGHLIGHTS/OBSERVATIONS

CAMPING LOG

LOG #

DATES

LOCATION

GPS COORDINATES/CAMPSITE # ______

ELEVATION/TERRAIN ______

WEATHER ______

______

ROUTE TAKEN TO CAMPSITE ______

______

FEES/PERMITS REQUIRED ______

PREFERRED SITE NUMBER(S) for next time ______

AMENITIES

- [ ] Parking | Number of vehicles ___
- [ ] Wheelchair accessibility
- [ ] Raised platform for tents
- [ ] Cell phone reception
- [ ] Campfire ring
- [ ] Grill
- [ ] Picnic table
- [ ] Firewood for sale

On-site trails: [ ] Biking [ ] Hiking [ ] ATV

Utility hook ups: [ ] Electric [ ] Water [ ] Sewer

Toilets: [ ] Pits [ ] Flush [ ] None

NOTES

MEALS

FLORA

FAUNA

HIGHLIGHTS/OBSERVATIONS

OVERALL RATING

CAMPING LOG

LOG #

DATES

LOCATION

GPS COORDINATES/CAMPSITE # ______

ELEVATION/TERRAIN ______

WEATHER ______

ROUTE TAKEN TO CAMPSITE ______

FEES/PERMITS REQUIRED ______

PREFERRED SITE NUMBER(S) for next time ______

AMENITIES

- [ ] Parking | Number of vehicles ___
- [ ] Wheelchair accessibility
- [ ] Raised platform for tents
- [ ] Cell phone reception
- [ ] Campfire ring
- [ ] Grill
- [ ] Picnic table
- [ ] Firewood for sale

On-site trails: [ ] Biking [ ] Hiking [ ] ATV

Utility hook ups: [ ] Electric [ ] Water [ ] Sewer

Toilets: [ ] Pits [ ] Flush [ ] None

NOTES

MEALS

FLORA

FAUNA

HIGHLIGHTS/OBSERVATIONS

CAMPING LOG

LOG #

DATES

LOCATION

GPS COORDINATES/CAMPSITE # ____

ELEVATION/TERRAIN ____

WEATHER ____

____

ROUTE TAKEN TO CAMPSITE ____

____

FEES/PERMITS REQUIRED ____

PREFERRED SITE NUMBER(S) for next time ____

AMENITIES

- [ ] Parking | Number of vehicles ___
- [ ] Wheelchair accessibility
- [ ] Raised platform for tents
- [ ] Cell phone reception
- [ ] Campfire ring
- [ ] Grill
- [ ] Picnic table
- [ ] Firewood for sale

On-site trails: [ ] Biking [ ] Hiking [ ] ATV

Utility hook ups: [ ] Electric [ ] Water [ ] Sewer

Toilets: [ ] Pits [ ] Flush [ ] None

NOTES

____

MEALS

FLORA

FAUNA

HIGHLIGHTS/OBSERVATIONS

CAMPING LOG

LOG #

DATES

LOCATION

GPS COORDINATES/CAMPSITE # ______

ELEVATION/TERRAIN ______

WEATHER ______

ROUTE TAKEN TO CAMPSITE ______

FEES/PERMITS REQUIRED ______

PREFERRED SITE NUMBER(S) for next time ______

AMENITIES

☐ Parking | Number of vehicles ___		☐ Wheelchair accessibility	
☐ Raised platform for tents		☐ Cell phone reception	
☐ Campfire ring	☐ Grill	☐ Picnic table	☐ Firewood for sale
On-site trails:	☐ Biking	☐ Hiking	☐ ATV
Utility hook ups:	☐ Electric	☐ Water	☐ Sewer
Toilets:	☐ Pits	☐ Flush	☐ None

NOTES

MEALS

FLORA

FAUNA

HIGHLIGHTS/OBSERVATIONS

NOTES & SKETCHES

"REAL FREEDOM LIES IN WILDNESS, NOT IN CIVILIZATION."

—Charles Lindbergh

"IN ALL THINGS OF NATURE THERE IS SOMETHING OF THE MARVELOUS."

—Aristotle

"EXPLORATION IS REALLY THE ESSENCE OF HUMAN SPIRIT."

—Frank Borman

"ALL NATURE WEARS ONE UNIVERSAL GRIN."

—Henry Fielding

"BETWEEN EVERY TWO PINE TREES THERE IS A DOOR LEADING TO A NEW WAY OF LIFE."

—John Muir

"IN WILDNESS IS THE PRESERVATION OF THE WORLD.'

—Henry David Thoreau

"IF PEOPLE SAT OUTSIDE AND LOOKED AT THE STARS EACH NIGHT, I'LL BET THEY'D LIVE A LOT DIFFERENTLY."

—Bill Watterson

"THERE IS NO CERTAINTY; THERE IS ONLY ADVENTURE."

—Roberto Assagioli

"NATURE IS OUR CHAPEL."

—Bjork

"I GO TO NATURE TO BE SOOTHED AND HEALED, AND TO HAVE MY SENSES PUT IN ORDER."

—John Burroughs

CAMPING CHECKLISTS

MY FAVORITE CAMPING TRIPS

EVERY MOMENT SPENT OUTSIDE IN NATURE IS PRICELESS, but some camping adventures are uniquely memorable. Perhaps it was the location, a particularly rewarding hike, or a gained sense of inner peace that made the trip stand out. Track your all-time favorites here.

DATE

LOCATION

HIGHLIGHTS

DATE

LOCATION

HIGHLIGHTS

DATE

LOCATION

HIGHLIGHTS

DATE

LOCATION

HIGHLIGHTS

DATE

LOCATION

HIGHLIGHTS

MY CAMPING BUCKET LIST

ALLOW YOUR SENSE OF ADVENTURE TO RUN WILD:
List any and every place you'd love to camp in your lifetime, whether it's on a parcel of public land in your home state or in the remote wilderness of another continent. Write them all down here and check them off as you go.

- [ ] ______
- [ ] ______
- [ ] ______
- [ ] ______
- [ ] ______
- [ ] ______
- [ ] ______
- [ ] ______
- [ ] ______
- [ ] ______
- [ ] ______
- [ ] ______
- [ ] ______
- [ ] ______
- [ ] ______
- [ ] ______
- [ ] ______
- [ ] ______
- [ ] ______
- [ ] ______

ESSENTIAL CAMPING GEAR

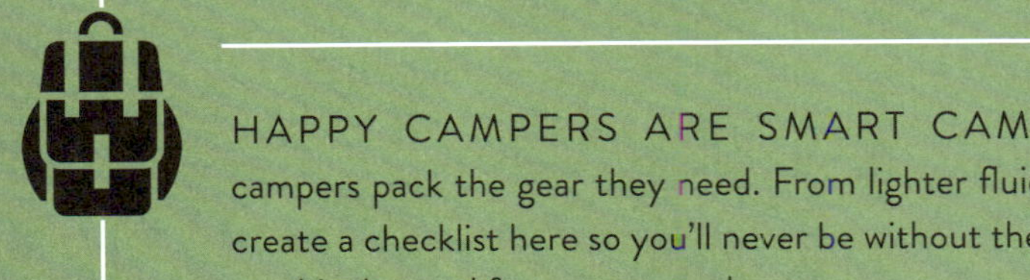

HAPPY CAMPERS ARE SMART CAMPERS, and smart campers pack the gear they need. From lighter fluid to a deck of cards, create a checklist here so you'll never be without the right supplies when you hit the road for your next adventure.

- [ ] ______
- [ ] ______
- [ ] ______
- [ ] ______
- [ ] ______
- [ ] ______
- [ ] ______
- [ ] ______
- [ ] ______
- [ ] ______
- [ ] ______
- [ ] ______
- [ ] ______
- [ ] ______
- [ ] ______
- [ ] ______
- [ ] ______
- [ ] ______
- [ ] ______

MEALS & FOOD PREPARATION

EVERYTHING TASTES BETTER OUTSIDE. On the left, keep a running list of your mess kit must-haves. On the right, write down your favorite campground meals, what ingredients they require, and preparation notes.

- [ ]
- [ ]
- [ ]
- [ ]
- [ ]
- [ ]
- [ ]
- [ ]
- [ ]
- [ ]
- [ ]
- [ ]
- [ ]
- [ ]
- [ ]
- [ ]
- [ ]
- [ ]
- [ ]
- [ ]
- [ ]

MEAL

INGREDIENTS

NOTES

MEAL

INGREDIENTS

NOTES

MEAL

INGREDIENTS

NOTES

MEAL

INGREDIENTS

NOTES

MEAL

INGREDIENTS

NOTES

NOTABLE WILDLIFE I'VE ENCOUNTERED

ALWAYS VIEW WILDLIFE FROM A SAFE DISTANCE. Remember, you're on their terrain now! Record the wild animals you've spotted while camping and any unique coloring, behaviors, or circumstances here.

ANIMAL	DATE	NOTES

WILDLIFE I'VE ENCOUNTERED

ANIMAL	DATE	NOTES

NOTABLE FLORA I'VE SEEN

PLANT LIFE IS A UNIQUE REFLECTION of the terrain you're camping in and can vary wildly from place to place. Record the flora you've discovered while camping, whether it's a patch of moss, a field of wildflowers, or a soaring redwood.

FLORA	DATE	NOTES

FLORA I'VE SEEN

FLORA	DATE	NOTES

THE CAMPER'S JOURNAL

weldonowen

www.weldonowen.com

ISBN: 978-1-68188-864-4

PRINTED IN CHINA

10 9 8 7 6 5 4 3

LIFE BEGINS AT THE
End
OF YOUR COMFORT
ZONE
1978
ADVENTURE
TIME
N
W
E
ALL GOOD THINGS
ARE WILD AND FREE
ADVENTURE AWAITS
AND I MUST GO